JAPAN

WESTVIEW PROFILES
NATIONS OF CONTEMPORARY ASIA

† Available in hardcover and paperback

JAPAN

A Postindustrial Power

THIRD EDITION, REVISED AND UPDATED

Ardath W. Burks

Westview Press

BOULDER • SAN FRANCISCO • OXFORD

952
B95j3

Westview Profiles / Nations of Contemporary Asia

Cover illustration: All Nippon Airways Hotel, Roppongi, Tokyo

All photos are courtesy of the Japan Information Center, Consulate General of Japan, 299 Park Avenue, New York, NY 10171.

Published in 1991 in the United States of America by Westview Press, Inc., 5500 Central Avenue, Boulder, Colorado 80301, and in the United Kingdom by Westview Press, 36 Lonsdale Road, Summertown, Oxford OX2 7EW

Library of Congress Cataloging-in-Publication Data
Burks, Ardath W.
  Japan : a postindustrial power / Ardath W. Burks.—3rd ed., rev. and updated.
    p. cm.—(Westview profiles. Nations of contemporary Asia)
  Includes bibliographical references (p.) and index.
  ISBN 0-8133-0989-1 (HC). — ISBN 0-8133-0990-5 (PB)
  1. Japan. I. Title. II. Series.
DS806.B85 1991
952.04—dc20   90-47953
                                                                    CIP

Printed and bound in the United States of America

The paper used in this publication meets the requirements of the American National Standard for Permanence of Paper for Printed Library Materials Z39.48-1984.

10   9   8   7   6   5   4   3   2   1

To Riki, my son,
who has provided me
with my own trans-Pacific bridge

Contents

Figures and Tables

Photographs

Preface to the Third Edition

Japan may well be the most progressive nation in the world. Indeed, if Japan does not offer "lessons for America," its intricately wrought and efficiently functioning society at the least deserves close attention. For some forty-five years, through travel and residence, research and teaching, it has been my privilege—only occasionally, frustration—to study Japan and the Japanese. Upon reflection, I have detected several subtle shifts in my own emphasis in scholarship and teaching. Two decades ago when I team-taught an introductory course on South and East Asia's great traditions and predominantly agrarian lifestyles, Japan already proved the interesting exception because a majority of the country's residents had begun to migrate to the large industrial cities.

More recently the concept of the postindustrial society has been the focus of my attention. As is explained in the text to follow, Japanese society is one in which the majority of the labor force is not only removed from primary (chiefly agricultural) pursuits, but also increasingly removed from secondary (industrial) employment and engaged in tertiary (service) activities. More and more, I have found it useful to relate metropolitan Tokyo to the greater metropolitan New York area: both are postindustrial societies. Today, many readers know little about rural America and even less about village Japan. In this context, the Japanese experiment is eminently worthy of study, not because many of the social formulas are directly transferable, but because Japanese attempts to come to grips with often intractable problems sometimes resemble, and sometimes contrast with, the efforts of other postindustrial powers, including the United States.

Although I have retired from teaching and administration since the appearance of the first edition (1981) of this volume, I have enjoyed the good fortune to remain involved in Japanese affairs. In the fall of 1982, prior to the appearance of the second edition (1984), I was in Japan doing research. In the fall of 1985, I had the privilege of serving as honorary chairman of the second international conference on foreign employees (*oyatoi*) in nineteenth-century Japan, held in Fukui. (The first conference had assembled at Rutgers University in 1967.) A preconference meeting of the U.S. delegation was held at the East-West Center, the University of Hawaii at Manoa. After the Fukui conference, my travels ranged from the Hokuriku region in the north to Kyūshū in the south.

During the summer of 1988, my wife and I were invited to join a delegation led by Mayor John A. Lynch of New Brunswick, N.J., a group that visited Tsuruoka and Fukui (sister cities of New Brunswick). In Tokyo the delegation was welcomed by Nakasone Hirofumi, member of the House of Councillors and son of the former prime minister (who was, at the time, in Moscow). During this trip, I was made more aware of the maturing of Japan as a high-technology society.

Anyone who works in, or does research on, Japan quickly accumulates a stock of obligations to cooperative Japanese. The author is no exception. During fourteen trips to East Asia (thirteen to Japan) in the postwar period, a large number of Japanese gave me and my family help, encouragement, and flawless hospitality. To professors emeriti Sakata Yoshio and Horie Yasuzō, my *sensei*, and Motoyama Yukihiko, my colleague, all of Kyoto University, and to other members of the Kindaika ("modernization") Seminar, I owe a debt for their patient attempts to introduce me to the views of Japanese scholars.

I wish to express gratitude specifically to the staff of the International House of Japan, Tokyo: the late chairman of the board, Dr. Matsumoto Shigeharu, and the present chairman, Dr. Nagai Michio; the managing director, Tanabe Tatsuro, whom I have known since 1952; and the librarian, Togasaki Tamiyo.

At the National Institute for Educational Research (the NIER, Kokuritsu Kyōiku Kenkyūjo), my former graduate research assistant and now colleague, Kaneko Tadashi, has provided me as regularly as the Japanese seasons with up-to-date statistical data for my annual contributions to encyclopedias, as well as information for this volume.

My university, Rutgers, enjoys a sister-institution tie with Fukui University. The president of that university, Shimada Tadashi, has been a generous host and understanding colleague. Thanks to Governor Kurita Yukio of Fukui-*ken* and to Mayor Otake Yukio of Fukui-*shi*, I have come to feel like an honorary citizen of the prefecture and city. I now understand a great deal more about local government in Japan from several visits to Fukui.

Here in the United States, for three decades I have received regular monthly inoculations of inspiration and enthusiasm from my colleagues in the University Seminar on Modern Japan, based at the East Asian Institute, Columbia University. Twice I have chaired the seminar, which draws scholars from as far north as Boston and as far south as Washington, D.C.

Vice Consul Mikami Yoichi of the Japan Information Center, Consulate General of Japan, New York, has given generously of his time to provide data, the Japanese viewpoint on issues, and the splendid illustrations in this volume.

As a member of the Japan Society, New York, I have profited from proximity to the Japan House, where I have attended well-organized programs, discussions, and seminars. I appreciate cooperation with Sandra Faux, Director of Publications, the Japan Society.

Several colleagues have read chapter drafts in the first, second, and third editions. Although, unfortunately, I am not a neighbor of Professor Emeritus David Kornhauser, University of Hawaii, our long and fruitful exchange of ideas (reflected in Chapter 1) has served to strengthen my grasp of Japan at ground level, so to speak. Professor Marius Jansen, Princeton University, was remarkably patient with my attempt to encapsulate the Japanese tradition (in Chapter 2). Vice President David Cayer, of Rutgers, and Elizabeth Cayer, who claim to be only amateur collectors of Japanese art, read the section on culture (Chapter 3). Professor Richard Wilson of Rutgers, a specialist on China and on political socialization, commented on the analysis of national character (Chapter 8). For data used in this section I am also indebted to Professor Nobuo Shimahara, my colleague in the Rutgers Graduate School of Education.

I was helped indirectly but immeasurably in writing updates of later chapters in the third edition by the fact that, for a decade, I have prepared annual reports on Japan for Political Risk Services, Inc. I have enjoyed an editorial relationship with Professor William Coplin, Syracuse University, one of the editors.

I remain grateful to a former colleague, Charles Ogrosky, for his care in rendering maps and charts.

Members of the efficient staff of Westview Press have been indefatigable in trying to improve drafts of all three editions. Mervyn Adams Seldon, Deborah Lynes, and Vicki Cooper worked on earlier editions; more recently Susan L. McEachern and Jeanne Campbell have lent support in producing the third edition.

Finally, at home, Jane Burks—"good wife and wise mother"—has subtly suggested improvements while pretending to help only with proofreading. In spite of all this help, some misinterpretations and errors undoubtedly remain in the text. For these I, of course, assume full responsibility.

In any book on Japan, the author and the reader encounter the problem of style in handling Japanese proper names. In most cases, as a courtesy to the Japanese, names are given according to their custom: that is, the surname first, with the given name following. In rare cases, the documentation of works by Japanese that have been translated into English and published in the West will show the name as it is listed (given name first, followed by family name). Most Americans of Japanese ancestry (*nisei* and *sansei*) prefer the Western style (given name first, followed by family name).

I have tried (for the general nonspecialist reader) to keep the use of Japanese words to a minimum. Even the casual reader, however, may wish to master some of the vocabulary and others (for example, advanced students in area-language studies) will want to note the Japanese terms for social phenomena.

Ardath W. Burks
Rutgers University

JAPAN

Introduction

This is a book about a land that was once—and indeed on occasion is still—regarded as exotic and "Oriental," Japan; and about a remarkably homogeneous people, the Japanese.

The Japanese no longer really live in the "Far East"; the term is an ethnocentric invention of the Europeans. Today Japanese reside in an area Americans might well call the "Middle West." In fact, Japanese now live throughout the world, in Southeast Asia, in Europe, in Latin America, and in the United States. For example, it is estimated that there are some 30,000 Japanese nationals working and residing in the metropolitan New York area. There may be even more in California. By one count there are about 80 Japanese firms located in New Jersey. Throughout the New York area there must be at least 500 Japanese restaurants.

If today's Japanese, unlike their ancestors who visited us in the nineteenth century, are not considered exotics, neither may they be considered familiar friends. As someone said, Americans and Japanese look at each other through opposite ends of a cultural telescope. This book is an attempt to bring Japan and the Japanese into sharper focus.

A description of the Japanese landscape is a logical beginning. Despite the depredations of industrialization and pollution, the proximity of mountains and sea still makes for startlingly beautiful scenery. The island nation is resource-poor, however, almost completely dependent on the outside world for resources and particularly for energy. Most Japanese live not in the celebrated villages, nor even in the cities, but in vast conurbations. Movement to the megalopolis in recent generations marks one of the significant migrations of our day. Yet the Japanese have a sense of continuity, the baggage of a long-lived tradition. Within that tradition is a finely tuned aesthetic sense, which, in turn, has guided the wonderful Japanese art.

In describing the Great Tradition and the Little Tradition of Japan, one encounters problems. Throughout there is need to balance culture

1

change (the persistence of a Japanese Way, yet its imperceptible alteration at home) with culture contact (the regular and dramatic confrontation with powerful influences from abroad). For example, how does one handle what has been called Japanese "feudalism"? Is it to be regarded as an isolated, backward, oppressive stage in the history of Japan? Are there "feudal residues" in Japanese society even today? Or, as former ambassador to Japan Edwin Reischauer and others do, should we think of the long period of Tokugawa peace (1603–1868) as in fact "post-feudal" or even "proto-modern," in short, as a preparation to withstand the impact of the nineteenth century and the West? Finally, how useful is the conceptual framework of modernization in explaining the social, economic, and political development directed first by the Meiji modernizers (1868–1912) and then by the aliens during the Occupation (1945–52) of Japan?

In any case, our contemporary neighbors, the Japanese, are themselves obsessed with a veritable fad of introspection. "Who are we Japanese?" they ask. There are various answers (some enlightened by scientific insight, some dangerous generalizations), replies that sometimes explain and sometimes exaggerate the complex social structure, intricate political culture, and vigorous economic behavior of the Japanese. The highly literate, well-informed Japanese are nonetheless not quite worldly. Acculturated within a unique society and facing formidable language barriers, they demonstrate an insularity that makes it difficult for them to do business abroad. Similarly, non-Japanese (*gaijin* or "outsiders") find it equally hard to do much more than tour Japan.

The cultural gap is most clearly revealed in the world's response to Japanese activities in foreign trade, investment abroad, and establishment of multinational branch plants outside Japan. Japan's need to trade for the sake of growth, its aggressive export policy, and its success, as measured by towering balance-of-payments surpluses, all create *real* economic issues between Japan and the other industrial democracies. The Japanese unusual capacity for work, unique commercial organization, and decision-making style, on the other hand, often create *unreal* fears about "the ugly Japanese," the superpower status of "Japan, Inc.," and the revival of Japanese imperialism.

Japan and the United States, for example, are now engaged in the largest bilateral cross-ocean trade in the history of the world. The Tokyo-Washington axis is marked by regular ministerial consultation, integrated security policies, and massive cultural and educational exchange. And yet Americans persist in thinking of Japanese as strange and exotic. To be fair, Japanese, too, carry around only caricatures of American life.

The Japanese experience is, on the one hand, a classic example of the movement from a primitive to a settled, agrarian—if preindustrial—

lifestyle. On the other hand, it represents a unique example of conversion from the traditional agrarian to the modern industrial style. Japan has been one of the first of the handful of countries to be "beyond modern." A majority of its labor force is now employed in the service, or tertiary, sector. This sector generates a larger proportion of the gross national product than do the primary (agricultural) and secondary (industrial) sectors. Finally, Japan's levels of capital accumulation and mass consumption now make possible a move from a labor-intensive or even capital-intensive stage to a knowledge-intensive stage.

Change has not, however, stopped at the tertiary level. In the 1980s vigorous debate marked another stage of development beyond modern, as "industrial restructuring" was matched by the further "internationalization" of Japanese society. Politics, political institutions, and political parties; economics, economic institutions, and labor-management negotiations; the society, social institutions, and social issues—all these display a cultural lag. Whether rooted firmly in nineteenth-century economic "struggle" or uprooted in the overwhelming "growth" since the 1960s, traditional Japanese organizations confront new problems as they face the costs of growth and new modes of citizen participation. Whether the disengaged in Japanese politics symbolize the end of ideology in this mass society remains an open question, but even tentative Japanese solutions should be of interest to citizens everywhere, especially to those who perceive the promise and peril of the technetronic age.

1

Sansui: The Landscape and Its Settlement

In Japanese art there is a venerable tradition called *sansui*. This term, which literally means "mountain and water," refers both to a style and to the visible, pleasing proximity of rounded hills, jagged peaks, calm bays, and tempestuous seas. Originally used to describe an inspiration for monochrome landscape painting, the term is also useful in summarizing the structure of the island nation.

STRUCTURE

The combination of mountains and sea in Japan has profoundly affected the historic development of the country and has contributed to the problem of human settlement faced by the Japanese even today. In brief, Japan is scenery-rich and resource-poor.

The Mountains

Geologists view the Japanese archipelago not so much as islands as immense mountains on the globe. These ranges rise 20,000 to 30,000 feet (6,100 to 9,100 meters) from the floor of the Pacific Ocean. Just east of, and close to, Japan is a deep trough, the Japan Trench, which at bottom reaches 36,198 feet (11,033 m) below sea level. Just to the south is another trough with a depth of more than 13,000 feet (4,000 m). On shore, Japan's mountains are sharply ridged; many of the peaks in central Honshū rise more than 10,000 feet (3,000 m) above sea level. Since glacial effects were not felt in this area, mountain slopes are quite steep and the valleys narrow, yet most of the terrain is forested hills.

Division of the country into relatively small plains (except where noted) may have contributed to the early clannishness of the Japanese and probably set the boundaries for old provinces. The topography, according to former ambassador Edwin O. Reischauer, may have also helped to shape the decentralized feudal pattern of medieval Japan. Until modern engineering enabled the building of rail lines, their cuts, bridges, and tunnels, and toll roads, lateral connections between the valleys were few. And sometimes, even today, topographical barriers have proved to be formidable. For example, in January 1979 the national railway system completed the world's longest tunnel on the Jōetsu superexpress line, beneath Mt. Tanigawa on the Gumma-Niigata prefectural border. At 13.7 miles (22 kilometers) in length, the Daishimizu Tunnel just surpassed the length of the Simplon Tunnel (12.3 miles or 20 km) on the Swiss-Italian alpine border.

In 1988 links were completed that more closely integrated two of Japan's more relatively isolated islands. In March, after more than twenty years of construction, the Seikan Tunnel opened for rail service between Hakodate on Honshū and Aomori on Hokkaidō. At just over 33 miles (53 km), it became the world's longest underseas passage. In April the Seto Ōhashi, a bridge over the Inland Sea, became the world's longest motor-rail span, connecting Kojima on Honshū with Sakaide on Shikoku.

Geographers do, of course, describe Japan as a series of festoon islands, stretching some 1,300 miles (2,100 km) from the Chishima (Kurile) island group in the northeast to the Nansei (Ryūkyū, including Okinawa) group in the southwest. (See Fig. 1.1.) In between, the archipelago consists of the four main islands—Hokkaidō, Honshū, Shikoku, and Kyūshū (97 percent of the total land area)—and of some 3,300 islets and rocks, many uncultivatable and uninhabited. Even when one thinks of Japan as an island-nation, it is difficult not to think of mountains.

Circum-Pacific crustal movements have formed and continue to shape the land, which is torn into bewildering fractions along fault lines, some heaped above and some sunk below the water. The resultant islands lie between a shallow submerged valley, the Sea of Japan, and a deep submerged depression, the Japan Trench.

Another explanation, borrowed from both geologists and geographers, has the Japanese islands poised precariously on a ring of fire. This zone of instability runs clear around, and borders on, the Pacific basin. In this sense, the islands are laid out in arcuate patterns, a series of convex bows. At the nodes in which the arcs intersect, there is direct or indirect evidence of volcanic activity. The four bows are:

1. *the Chishima* (Kurile) *arc:* anchored in the central Hokkaidō node (recent volcanic eruptions occurred at the site of the 1972 Winter Olympic games, near Sapporo)
2. *the Honshū arc:* anchored in the north on the western peninsula of Hokkaidō and in the south in the Kyūshū node

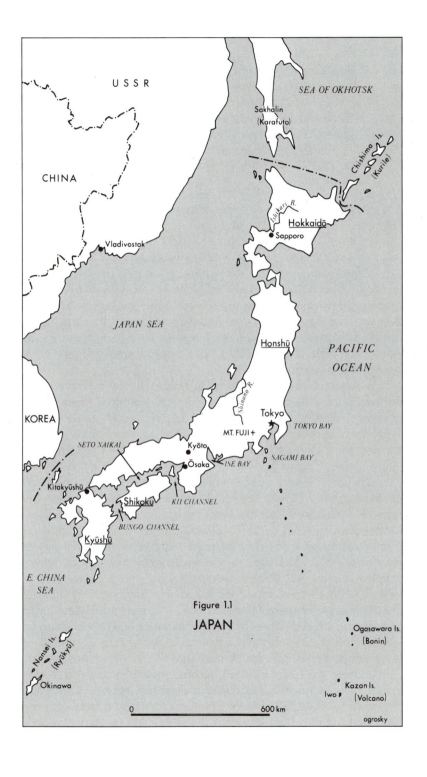

USSR

SEA OF OKHOTSK

Sakhalin
(Karafuto)

Chishima Is.
(Kurile)

CHINA

Ishikari R.

Hokkaidō

Sapporo

Vladivostok

JAPAN SEA

Honshū

PACIFIC
OCEAN

Shinano R.

KOREA

Tokyo

MT. FUJI +

TOKYO BAY

SETO NAIKAI

Kyōto

Ōsaka

ISE BAY

SAGAMI BAY

Kitakyūshū

Shikoku

KII CHANNEL

BUNGO CHANNEL

Kyūshū

E. CHINA
SEA

Figure 1.1

JAPAN

Ogasawara Is.
(Bonin)

Nansei Is.
(Ryūkyū)

Okinawa

Kazan Is.
Iwo
(Volcano)

0   600 km

ogrosky

3. *the Nansei* (Ryūkyū) *arc:* anchored in Kyūshū (including Mt. Aso, an active volcano and the world's largest caldera type)
4. *the Ogasawara* (Bonins) *arc:* anchored in the north on the Izu Peninsula of Honshū and running south through the Izu, Ogasawara (Bonin), and Kazan (Volcano) islands (including Mt. Fuji, 12,389 feet [3,776 m] above sea level, a volcano that last erupted in 1707)

The active and extinct volcanoes within Japan total 265. Scientists have estimated the total number of eruptions in the world during the historic age at about 540. Japan accounted for 30 before 1900, and about 20 in this century (or about 10 percent of the total).

Cross-island tectonic zones have given rise to spectacular scenery and have contributed to instability. Another result is that in the nineteenth century Japan gave birth to the science of seismology. In modern times, delicate seismographs have recorded more than 5,000 earthquakes annually in Japan. About one in five has been detectable by humans. About one-fifth of these (200) have been strong enough to stop the swing of a pendulum.

The major earthquake zone is related to the volcanic nodes. It is on the Pacific side, between the archipelago and the Japan Trench, and epicenters tend to be on the slopes of the Trench at depths of about 3,300 feet (1,000 m) below sea level. The Japanese have lent the world a name for a frequent and feared earthquake by-product, the seismic "tidal" wave (*tsunami*).

The greatest earthquake in modern Japanese history, which occurred on September 1, 1923, leveled Tokyo and its environs, leaving more than 130,000 dead. Today, the Japanese have become fatalistically adjusted to the idea that great quakes will occur. In 1975, an earthquake forecast council estimated that a Richter-scale-5 quake would cause suffering for more than 133,000 citizens in the southwestern wards of Tokyo; water supply to some 420,000 houses in Tokyo would be interrupted; and some 15,000 citizens would be killed in Kawasaki City, just south of Tokyo. In spite of these forecasts, with the most up-to-date engineering and a considerable dose of faith, Tokyoites have continued to erect towering office buildings and have expanded vast underground networks of subways, pedestrian malls, and shops.

Indeed, the Japanese have become so inured to nature's might that in the 1970s a novel titled *Nihon chimbotsu* (Japan sinks)[1] was widely read with fear and fascination. The work, actually a *social science* fiction, described the effect on society if the whole archipelago was doomed to slide into the ocean after a tectonic shift.

This is not to say that natural disasters have offered no blessings. As a result of volcanic activity and earthquakes, Japan has magnificent natural scenery: the perfect cone of Fuji-*san*, the cauldron of Aso, volcanic bays in Hokkaidō, and the hot springs that dot the islands.

The Seacoast

The coasts of Japan are also, in effect, mere adjuncts to the mountainous structure. Capes, headlands, peninsulas with their lighthouses, and the bays between are either protrusions of, or submerged valleys between, the pervasive mountains. Japanese tend to think of their country as "a small, narrow, island nation." In fact, no part of Japan is more than seventy miles from a coast, and all of the country lies in the shadows of mountains.

The total area of the four main islands is about 145,883 square miles (377,837 km^2). There is a total length of shoreline of about 9,800 miles (15,800 km). Japan thus has 1 linear mile of coast per 14 square miles of land (as compared to Britain's ratio of 1:8).

The magnificent Setonaikai (literally, "sea within channels," or the Inland Sea) is actually a submerged shallow structural depression nestled between the mountains of Shikoku and the less rugged highlands of western Honshū. The line of fracture is fringed by a chain of volcanoes (all extinct except Mt. Aso on Kyūshū) and more than 950 islands. Some one-half million acres (202,500 hectares) of shores surrounding the Inland Sea have been declared national park in hopes of protecting the legendary beauty of the region. The main western water highway is well known to the Japanese, historically having served as the connection between the parts of Kyūshū that were points of contact with the continent of Asia and the oldest settled culture in the Yamato Basin, around Nara. As geographer David Kornhauser has described them, the coastal plains on Honshū face south and west just like the porch and sliding doors of a classic Japanese farmhouse. Shifting the image, the Setonaikai is Japan's Mediterranean with a pleasingly mild climate.

Today one can easily forget the long and relatively quiet coastline facing north and west over the Japan Sea. Japan's "backside" (*ura Nihon*), it has quite different topography and sharply different climate. It can therefore be a delight to the infrequent tourist who travels west to Matsue, where Lafcadio Hearn lived and died, or who journeys northwest to the undisturbed "Little Kyoto," Kanazawa. Older Japanese remember pre–World War II days, however, when this coast linked Japan with its interests on the continent—in Manchuria, Korea, and North China. There are still important ports in the area. One is Niigata, which was used in the 1950s to repatriate Koreans.

Geography, climate, and recent history have made the Pacific, or eastern and southeastern, coasts vastly more important. The major bays, really submerged valleys, used for shipping Japan's exports are here. They are (ranging southwest) Tokyo (including the port of Yokohama), Sagami, Ise, and Ōsaka, including the port of Kōbe. Mention must also be made of the portals of the Setonaikai, the Bungo Channel to the west, and the Kii Channel to the east. There are new port cities all along the Setonaikai and harbors serving the modern industrial complex located on northern Kyūshū. Perhaps more important in history are the other large bays in Kyūshū, serving Nagasaki, Sasebo, and Kagoshima.

The peninsulas that jut into, and the bays that welcome, the Pacific Ocean enjoy the warm flow of the Kuroshio (the Black, or Japan, Current). It serves the same function as does its sister stream along the California coast, namely, to moderate the climate of all neighboring areas. Thus, climate and accessibility have encouraged the growth of great cities and the expansion of ports (and consequently the mainstream of history) to be on the Pacific side. The post–World War II development of Japan to superpower status, linked through the Pacific basin to the Americas and to Western Europe, has accelerated the trend, making this region domestically a great urban corridor and internationally Japan's window to the world.

The Plains Between

In Japan, then, the seacoast is nearby, and throughout almost all the land, mountains are visible. The compact character of the habitable remainder is possibly the explanation for the Japanese love of landscapes and the tendency to reproduce them on a small scale, for example, in tiny trees (*bonsai*) and in miniature gardens.

It follows that level land has always been at a premium: traditionally, as a base for rice culture; currently, as a base for industrial and postindustrial cities. *Only about one-quarter of the total area of Japan has land with slopes less than fifteen degrees;* only 24 percent of Honshū, the most populated island, is so constructed. Lowlands make up only about one-eighth of the total area, and a large proportion of these are eroded deposits from the highlands. Thus, Japan's lowlands, too, are mere adjuncts to the mountains.

There are only a few relatively large plains, and these, of course, loom large in Japan's history. They include the Kantō, which hosts the modern Tokyo metropolitan area; the Nobi, which is occupied by Nagoya and its industrial environs; the Tsukushi, which holds the manufacturing cities of northern Kyūshū; and the Ishikari and the Tokachi, which contain Sapporo and the developing regions of Hokkaidō. None of these, it should be noted, is anywhere near the size of the immense North China Plain.

As a result of the topography, Japan's rivers tend to be short and, in rainy season, fast flowing. There are only two rivers over 200 miles (320 km) in length: the Ishikari in Hokkaidō and the Shinano in central Honshū. Fourteen rivers are between 100 and 200 miles (160 and 320 km) in length; eight, less than 100 miles long. None of the rivers plays a role in Japanese life equivalent to that of the Yangtse in China, the Mississippi in the United States, or the Amazon in South America.

Japanese tend to think of their country as being quite small. Japan is about 10 percent smaller than the U.S. state of California, with which it is most often compared. The country is larger in area, however, than any of the European nations except Sweden, France, and Spain. In latitudinal spread it is quite elongated, stretching (in the American imagination) from Hokkaidō (between Montreal and Boston) in the north through northern Honshū (Philadelphia), Tokyo (North Carolina), Ōsaka (South Carolina), and southern Kyūshū (the Florida panhandle), to Okinawa (Gulf of Mexico) in the south. Until recently, a south-to-north journey between Fukuoka and Sapporo took more than 20 hours by rail, even with the speedy sector on bullet trains of the New Tōkaidō Line (six hours from Fukuoka to Tokyo). New bullet-train service from Tokyo to Sendai and planned extension via Aomori to Sapporo will soon cut the time in half.

By jet aircraft, if schedules were so fitted, it would still take three hours to fly from Kyūshū to Hokkaidō. In longitudinal width Japan is narrow, but cross-Honshū travel is hindered by the fact that lateral rail connections are widely spaced. Central Honshū terrain is rugged, and rail traffic across it is slow because most of the connections are single-track lines. (In October 1978, the government approved plans for completion of five new superexpress rail lines over the next decade, which will increase both vertical and lateral connections.)

Distances and space are relative, of course, to the state of the art in transportation technology. Sometimes (as will be seen in an examination of human settlement below), social change and government decree set the boundaries of districts. Nonetheless, the Japanese have tended to think of certain regions in rather traditional fashion. Viewed geographically and in terms of early history, such regions still make sense in light of the placement of mountain barriers, stretches of seacoast, and narrow valleys. They include:

Northeast Japan:	*Hokkaidō* ("northern sea road")
	Tōhoku ("northeast")
Central Japan:	*Kantō* ("east of the pass")
	Tōkai ("east, or Pacific, coast")
	Hokuriku ("north, or Japan Sea, shore")
	Tōsan ("eastern highlands")
Southwest Japan:	*Kinki* ("near boundaries," or old home provinces; also *Kansai*, "west of the pass")
	Chūgoku ("middle realm")
	Sanin ("shady, or north, side of mountains")
	Sanyō ("sunny, or south, side of mountains")
	Shikoku ("four provinces" [island name])
	Kyūshū ("nine provinces" [island name])

CLIMATE

The mountains, the seas, and the relative location of the plains between them do, of course, work their effects on Japan's climate. And naturally, the latitudinal range is influential. Thus, Hokkaidō's climate is boreal, Tokyo's is temperate, and Okinawa's is subtropical. The major sources of the country's weather cycles, however, are really external. In the broader sense, they are continental and maritime in origin. There are three major air masses to which, over the years, Japanese have become acclimated.

The first is the Siberian polar continental high, or northwest monsoon, of winter. This air mass supplies initially cold and dry winds that are modified into warmer, moist, and unstable currents, particularly over the Japan Sea coast. The result is exactly like that found in the snow shadow east of the Great Lakes of North America. In fact, there is probably more snow cover on the northwest Japan Sea coastal region than is found in any equally populous area of the world. The environment's "atmosphere" has been captured by Nobel Prize winner Kawabata Yasunari in his novel *Yukiguni* (Snow country).[2]

For the rest of Japan, during winter the northwest monsoon provides dry weather and bright sunshine during the day and snapping cold, owing to lack of radiation, at night. Even high areas in Kyūshū may see some snow, but it melts promptly. Some yearly averages include 3 days of snow for Ōsaka; 8 days, Tokyo; 42 days, Sendai; 82 days, Niigata; and 132 days (December through early April) for Sapporo on Hokkaidō. The heaviest fall of all occurs around Takata, directly north of Tokyo on the Japan Sea coast, with as much as 26.5 inches (70 cm.) on a single day.

Snow country: Prefectures on the Japan Sea are famous for winter snows.

The second major air mass that profoundly affects Japan is the Ogasawara tropical oceanic low, or southeast monsoon, of summer. This generates southeasterlies and pours heat and humidity over Tokyo Bay and into Tokyo, just as the summer circulation around Bermuda pumps humid heat over Chesapeake Bay and into Washington, D.C. There is considerably less difference in climate between the two sides of Honshū in summer than in winter. Summers on the Japan Sea coasts can be quite warm but are less humid than those on the Pacific side.

The third major system is the Okhotsk polar oceanic high, which in the June-July period flows down from the north and confronts the Ogasawara system coming up from the south. The result is that for about 30 days (in most areas except for Hokkaidō) there is a front of stagnation, with soft winds and high humidity, gloomy skies, and rainy weather. Dense clouds filter the sunshine, and Japanese refer to this period as "the season of mold." Ample precipitation, called "plum rains" (*baiu*), comes precisely in the warm growing season and makes possible the traditional, intensive garden or hothouse agriculture.

Similar monsoonal shifts in the August-October period result in the other familiar natural disaster (besides earthquakes)—the typhoons (*taifū*, literally, "great winds"). These sweep up through "typhoon alley," Okinawa. If the Japanese are lucky, these storms only brush the southern and eastern Pacific coast; but on occasion they are accompanied by torrential rains and slam into the heavily populated regions of Kyūshū and Honshū.[3]

Since the changes in weather have been fairly regular, they have been translated by Japanese into traditional life cycles, planting and harvesting seasons, and religious rituals. These in turn mark subtle subdivisions of seasons. The old lunar calendar, which was used until 1872, recognized twenty-four subseasons in a year, including "beginning of spring," "appearance of worms," "opening of summer," "little heat," "great heat," "beginning of autumn," "cold dew," "opening of winter," "little cold," and "great cold."

Just as the mountain spine on Honshū divides Japan, so latitude provides a useful dividing line of the country. Above about 37° north latitutde (and at higher elevations even in central Japan), winters are too cold and long for double cropping. Below this latitude there are usually two crops: irrigated rice in summer and a dry crop in winter. The growing season ranges from less than 150 days in Hokkaidō to as much as 300 days in the warmest parts of the south. Climate has been linked with the history of settlement: in the north, farms appeared later than in central and southern Japan. The north remains less densely populated, and farms there are much larger (10 to 12 acres [4 to 5 ha] in Hokkaidō) than those in the south since it takes more land to support one household.

Within moderate limits, Japan has a variety of climates; average temperature and humidity reflect latitude and the movement of air masses in fairly regular patterns (as shown in Table 1.1). Ordinary Japanese mark the change of seasons in a more mundane fashion: when to shed long (winter) underwear and put on short (summer) garments, and when to shift from drinking warm sake (winter) to drinking cold beer (summer). Another familiar sign (of spring) is the appearance of the beloved cherry blossoms. Any Japanese can tell you within a few days the traditional date when the blossoms appear for any region. In more scientific terms, the blooms—a symbol of Japan—appear when the average daytime temperature reaches 50° F (10° C). Thus, isochronal lines (as shown in Figure 1.2) reinforce tradition and clearly show the march of spring from southwest to northeast Kyūshū-Shikoku, end of March; central Honshū-Kantō, April 10; north-central Honshū, April 20; Tōhoku, April 30; and Hokkaidō, May 10.

A less aesthetic and more practical means by which Japanese mark the seasons is their use of either heating or cooling. The Japan Meteorological Agency has garnered statistics that indicate heating is required for dwellings from mid-October to the end of April in Hokkaidō; from the end of November to mid-March in Tokyo; and from mid-December

TABLE 1.1   Average Temperature and Precipitation

Month	Sapporo		Tokyo		Kagoshima	
January	−6°C	100mm	2°C	40mm	7°C	65mm
February	−5	70	3	70	8	110
March	−2	60	6	100	10	150
April	5	55	12	150	15	200
May	10	50	17	150	18	220
June	15	50	20	175	23	400
July	20	80	25	130	27	330
August	22	100	30	140	27	225
September	17	150	22	240	22	200
October	10	125	15	235	16	110
November	3	130	15	200	13	80
December	−3	110	10	80	8	80

Source: Ryuziro Isida, *Geography of Japan* (Tokyo: Kokusai Bunka Shinkokai, 1961), p. 28.

to the end of February in southern Kyūshū. Air-conditioning is never needed in Hokkaidō. It is desirable for about 20 days during August in northeast Honshū; for about 65 days from mid-July to early September in Tokyo; and for 75 days from early July to mid-September in Kyūshū.

THE JAPANESE

One might well wonder why there should be a description of the Japanese people in a chapter devoted to basic geography. Yet the relationship of the people of Japan to their land is unique. Both are so intertwined that it is doubtful that a cultural group anywhere else has had such an impact on defining its own part of the earth. Moreover, although the Japanese, too, like to think back to their simiple, rustic, and natural environment, scarcely a portion of Japan has not been subtly shaped by the human beings who have for so long inhabited the island nation.

Irrigated paddy fields for wet rice culture have been in existence since the Japanese came across the edge of history. Terraced plots have marched up the lower mountains slopes to catch water from the reservoirs above. The hillsides have hosted rice, vegetables, and tea. More than two-thirds of Japan's area is covered by forests and, at first glance, these seem to be primeval. In fact, the woods have been cut innumerable times. Present stands are products of abundant rainfall and scientific management by humans. On level ground, of course, Japanese have used and misused every available inch of land. They have cut into the mountains in back of Kōbe, using the fill to extend the plain. Bodies

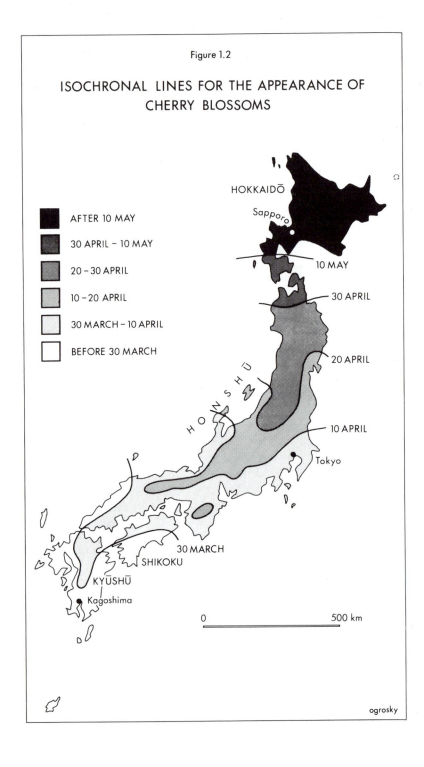

Figure 1.2

ISOCHRONAL LINES FOR THE APPEARANCE OF
CHERRY BLOSSOMS

AFTER 10 MAY

30 APRIL – 10 MAY

20 – 30 APRIL

10 – 20 APRIL

30 MARCH – 10 APRIL

BEFORE 30 MARCH

HOKKAIDŌ

Sapporo

10 MAY

30 APRIL

20 APRIL

10 APRIL

Tokyo

HONSHŪ

30 MARCH

SHIKOKU

KYŪSHŪ

Kagoshima

0   500 km

ogrosky

of water, like Kojima Bay in Okayama, have been diked to make more land. Much of the western side of Tokyo Bay, from Tokyo through Kawasaki down to Yokohama, has been reclaimed from the sea. The Organization for Economic Cooperation and Development (OECD) has reported that Japan is the only country with comprehensive zoning nationwide. In 1968, the entire country was divided into three land use zones: agricultural, urban, and other. In Japan, people have long been part of the landscape.

People of the Plains

Although Japan's total population is dwarfed by that of China, India, the Soviet Union, or the United States, again the Japanese are not really a small group. In 1979 and again in 1986 summit leaders of seven advanced industrial nations were convened in Tokyo. Of the nations represented, Japan was twice the size of each of the European partners in population (West Germany, France, Great Britain, and Italy), almost five times the size of Canada, and about one-half the size of the United States.

From the end of the sixteenth century up to the 1860s, the population remained fairly stable. Until modern times the total never exceeded 30 million; the standard Asian pattern of high birth but also high death rates set limits to growth. Even so, in the 1700s Japan's population (25 million) exceeded that of France, which had the largest population in Europe.

Beginning in 1868 with the modernization that marked the Meiji period, although the birthrate remained high, the death rate began to decline dramatically. By 1900 the total population had reached 44 million. Reliable census data compiled every five years thereafter revealed a quinquennial increase of anywhere from 5 to 8 percent in the years 1900–35 and an estimated total population of 69.3 million in 1935. As might be expected, the 5-year *rate* of increase showed a drastic decline in Japan's war years (1935–40, 3.87 percent; 1940–45, 0.30 percent). Then the next five years brought the celebrated "baby boom" (1945–50, 15.32 percent), which resulted in a total population of 83.2 million by 1950. Thereafter, strong social measures (including legalized abortion) and a taste of affluence have slowed the growth rate to about 0.45 percent annually. Even such a low rate, however, has still produced a net yearly increase of more than 600,000 because of the large population base (estimated at 123,130,000 in July 1989). Experts have predicted that Japan will reach equlibrium in the year 2005 at about 129 million.

Indeed, it is now quite clear that the interesting population issues in Japan lie not in questions of quantity—sheer numbers—but of quality, the age structure, distribution of the total, and employment of the labor force. A good deal more attention will be devoted to these problems in Chapters 6 and 7. It will suffice here to cite a few illustrations.

For example, although the *rate* of increase in Japan's total population has declined steadily, on occasion certain sectors have increased dramatically. Thus, in the spring of 1978 an unprecedented total of more than 2 million first-grade pupils flooded the elementary schools. These were, of course, the children of the baby-boom generation of thirty years before. In somewhat similar fashion, because of the very high health standards in Japan and concomitant longevity, the population has shown signs of aging rapidly. The "graying" of Japan had already resulted, in the late 1980s, in 11 percent of the total population being sixty-five years of age or older. Estimates have projected the percentage at 23.4 percent of the total in the year 2020, far surpassing the population reached in other advanced industrial nations. Finally, there has been, of course, a sharp shift in distribution of the population across the landscape of Japan, from rural areas (and primary pursuits in agriculture, forestry, and fishing) to metropolitan regions (secondary and tertiary pursuits in industry and services). This move has constituted one of the great migration of modern times.

In this last sense, too, Japan is not among the small but among the large countries. Gross figures for population density tend to be misleading. The overall average is 710 people per square mile, less than that of the Netherlands, three times that of West Germany, and almost five times that of Great Britain. The only comparable figures are those for unusual neighbors of Japan, which are in fact city-states—Hong Kong and Singapore.

The Settlements

Geographers tend to use the term "settlements," but often find themselves puzzling (particularly since 1960) over how to explain the differences among governmental units, traditional and modern metropolitan regions, and actual (settled) areas in Japan. Let us sort out these distinctions in very general terms.

First, there are 47 major administrative divisions of the total area of Japan: 42 rural prefectures (*-ken*), including Okinawa; 2 urban prefectures (*-fu*), Ōsaka and Kyōto; the metropolitan-capital prefecture (*-to*), Tokyo; and 1 district (*-dō*), Hokkaidō. Thus one speaks of rural Shimane-*ken*; of the traditional capital, Kyōto-*fu*; of the modern capital, Tōkyō-*to*; and of the island-district, Hokkaidō. As of March 1988, the entire area of all of these major divisions was subdivided into 3,246 administrative units. These included 591 villages (*-mura*), 2,000 towns (*-machi*), and 655 cities (*-shi*).

It is perhaps easier to return to the concept of settlements. This is because the legal units, cities, towns, villages—even metropolitan Tokyo—have embraced, since 1953, farmlands, forests, mountainous areas, and even (in the case of Tōkyō-*to*) remote islets. In that year such areas were incorporated in an amalgamation of administrative units. Similarly, on the other extreme, within villages (-*mura*) there are still smaller, extralegal settlements called hamlets (*buraku*). These are basic collections of 10 to 100 farm households—functionally agrarian settlements built around the planting and harvesting of rice, the rice cooperative, and irrigation projects.

Although they encompass agricultural lands, the small towns are not completely artificial units in that their core populations (10,000 to 20,000) do constitute marketplaces for surrounding rural areas. The cities, with their core populations (20,000 to 50,000), also make up local centers for commerce, industry, and administration. Finally, even the largest legal units only roughly delineate the actual urban settlements. Modern demographers use another term, the "densely inhabited district" (DID), to arbitrarily demark areas containing 10,000 persons per square mile. Although in the 1970s such areas accounted for only 1.25 percent of Japan's total area, they already housed more than 47 million persons, or almost half the total population of Japan.

This chapter will pay somewhat greater attention to the dwindling rural areas, closer to the original landscape, and somewhat less to the booming urban regions, imposed on the landscape by man. The latter will be discussed in greater detail in the chapters on modernization, the Japanese personality, the economy, and postindustrial society in Japan. To describe these two different kinds of human settlement, Fred Riggs has coined two descriptive terms, agraria and industria, which go beyond the obvious—agricultural as compared with industrial pursuits—and highlight variable lifestyles.

Agraria. Despite the fact that by 1965 the population in what might be called agrarian households had fallen below the 30 million mark, the rural origins of most people remained significant in the Japanese mental set. And although the proportion of labor force applied to agricultural work has declined to 9 percent (May 1988), the Japanese have persisted in emphasizing the rustic and traditional in their village background. The outlook is somewhat similar to that of Americans who persist in watching their late-night television dramas to harken back to a long-eliminated frontier.

To those who have never had to labor in the milieu—foreign tourists and city-bred Japanese—village Japan still holds great charm. Historians believe that rice culture, probably imported from South China, arrived

Computerized rice cultivator

at least as early as the second century A.D. The Japanese have been cultivating rice ever since.

Into the small dike-bordered paddy, as level as a pool table in order to distribute water evenly, rice has perennially been transplanted from carefully tended seedbeds near the farmhouse. This has traditionally been a labor-intensive project, small-scale horticultural agriculture. It was not efficient in terms of hourly labor input, but in output per acre it has remained the most productive in the world. (Late in 1978, two months after Japan signed a treaty of peace and friendship with China, the former moved to repay an historic debt. Tokyo signed a further agreement in Beijing promising to send eight Japanese agricultural experts to North China to teach local farmers how to grow high-yield rice in cold climates.)

In modern times, production has been heightened by intensive application of fertilizer: at first, nightsoil from the urban areas, and later, chemicals. A steady decline in labor force was thus offset by an agricultural revolution, which also saw an invasion of the paddies by machines. In the 1950s in villages throughout Japan, Japanese began to use a one-cycle plow called the bean (*mame*) cultivator because of its size and shape. Today, according to polls conducted by the Office of the Prime Minister, rice remains *the* staple food in Japanese diets: for

71 percent of the respondents at breakfast, for 77 percent at lunch, and for 96 percent at dinner. As a result, some 40 percent of Japan's total cultivated area is in rice; 99.5 percent of the rice fields is in wet paddies.

Noodles in a variety of styles have always been popular, and bread, in an increasingly mobile society, has grown in favor. The demand for wheat and barley has therefore increased, and more than four times the domestic wheat supply has to be imported.

Fruit as dessert appeals to Japanese and has become a premium cash crop, but costs have outpaced inflation of other food prices. Apples are grown in the north; pears, grapes, melons, and mandarin oranges in the south. Tea is grown mainly in Shizuoka, but many areas in the south and even in the mountains boast of local brands, which are prized as souvenirs by urbanites returning from the countryside.

Animal husbandry traditionally has not been a prominent pursuit, except for cattle introduced into Hokkaidō in the nineteenth century and for the celebrated hand-tended Kōbe beef (with appropriately pro- hibitive prices). Chickens and pigs have constituted the main livestock supply. Goats have been practically household pets.

It is no surprise to learn that in recent times some members of rural households have left home entirely during slack seasons, seeking employment in seasonal deep-sea fishing, or, in light industry farther south. In such households the average total membership (5.1) simply cannot be supported by the average number engaged in agricultural work (1.8). Put another way, only about one in seven farmers cultivates plots of more than 3.5 acres (1.42 ha) (whereas 3.7 acres are required for a living). Finally, four-fifths of all Japanese farmers are engaged in supplemental occupations in nearby cities.

If the first historically visible settled Japanese were agriculturalists on the plains, the very first archaeologically identified Japanese were fishermen on the seas. With an unusual occurrence of warm and cool ocean currents just offshore, Japan has traditionally depended on products from the sea for a major portion of its protein. Rapid industrialization after the war, together with headlong neglect, has resulted in contam- ination of the Inland Sea. Its condition has become as bad as that of the eastern Great Lakes in the United States, and other nearby waters have also felt the effects of pollution. Despite the growing scarcity of nearby fish and the toll of inflation, the national taste for seafood continues unabated. Japanese commercial fishermen have therefore roamed the seas widely. Japanese have led the world in range of operations, variety of fish taken, and total catch (more than 12.4 million metric tons in 1987). At home, Japanese husband the seas as farmers husband the land, planting, for example, varieties of seaweed. In rivers and reservoirs throughout Japan freshwater fish are cultivated.

High-rises in Shinjuku, site of the Tokyo Metropolitan Government headquarters

Industria. Although, as has been noted, many Japanese like to think of their culture as one directly descended from rural, agrarian antecedents, many of the so-called traditional Japanese values, it may be argued, emanated from towns. Most Japanese, it is true, are only one or two generations removed from the agrarian village; many Japanese, however, can trace ancestry to a number of generations who were resident in towns and even cities. These were what Gideon Sjoberg has called preindustrial cities.

In the postwar era, the Japanese have established a number of brand new industrial centers. Most of Japan's cities, however, rest on foundations of traditional urban settlements. There are, for example, those that are descended from classic metropolitan capitals laid out according to imperial plan (*jōbo*), Kyōto and Nara; from temple towns (*monzen machi*) like Nagano; from stage towns (*shukuba machi*) like Hamamatsu; and, of course, from the celebrated castle towns (*jōka machi*) like Sendai, Kanazawa, Edo, Nagoya, Ōsaka, Himeji, Okayama, Hiroshima, and Kagoshima. Edo (modern Tokyo) was the largest city in the world around 1700. Granted, most of the castles (except for the magnificent "White Heron" of Himeji) were crystal-clear zero aiming points for bombardment during the war and subsequently have had to be reconstructed in reinforced concrete made to look like wood.

Today, of course, the Japanese city is the true center of Japanese culture. The majority of Japanese, as we shall see, live in cities. The dwindling few who may be regarded as rural dwellers have one foot in the city. For everyone, city standards are relayed through ubiquitous mass communication (*masu komi*, as the Japanese call it). City-produced and city-distributed goods and services are now available throughout the country.

At the peak of secondary industrial development in the 1960s, Japan had already created an urban heartland, a narrow coastal band running 600 miles from northeast to southwest. This corridor contained all of Japan's cities with a population of 1 million or more. They included the capital, Tokyo (already with 10 percent of the total population of Japan), and neighboring Yokohama; Nagoya and the Ōsaka-Kyōto-Kōbe complex; somewhat smaller cities along the Inland Sea; and the industrial concentrations of northern Kyūshū.

The reasons for urban concentration at this manufacturing stage were quite clear: The area was responsible for over 75 percent of all industrial production; it was served by the major ports, an essential factor for the import of raw materials and for the export of finished goods; the corridor had the most efficiently developed transportation network; and its cities housed the skilled labor force. Later in the 1970s, especially after the passage of environmental laws, deconcentration of industry began to make more sense. By that time, however, Japanese cities had entered yet another stage, which seemed to justify even greater concentration. That phenomenon is more fully described in Chapter 7.

To return to the demographers' term, densely inhabited district, by 1960, 43.7 percent of the population lived in DIDs; in 1965, the total reached 48.1 percent; and in 1970, 53.5 percent of all Japanese were in DIDs. Tokyo, viewed in this light, was one vast DID, with a total population (1985 census) of 27,824,000 (within a 50-kilometer [31-mile] radius from the Tōchō, the Tokyo Metropolitan Government head-quarters). Japanese have come to know the area as Keihin, using the Chinese variant pronunciation of elements of the cities' names (Tokyo-Yokohama).

Second only to the Tokyo metropolitan region was Ōsaka and its neighbors (known to Japanese as Hanshin [Ōsaka-Kōbe] or sometimes as Keihanshin [Kyōto-Ōsaka-Kōbe]). In 1985 the DID population of the area was 15,891,000 (within a 50-kilometer radius from Ōsaka city hall). The whole region facing Ōsaka Bay stretched as far south as Wakayama; west of Ōsaka it included the steel mills and distilling plants of Amagasaki and Nishinomiya; farther west it embraced Japan's largest port, Kōbe (1,411,000); and to the north within commuting range it included the splendid traditional capital and modern bedroom-community of Kyōto (1,479,000).

Next in size came Nagoya and its environs (known as the Chūkyō region). In 1985 the DID population of this area was 8,139,000 (within a 50-kilometer radius from the Nagoya city hall). Settlements fanned out from this core and embraced petrochemical production in Yokkaichi to the southwest; automobile plants in Kariya and Toyota to the southeast; ceramics in Seto, Kasugai, and Kajima to the northeast; and textile mills in Ichinomiya and Gifu to the northwest.

The metropolitan region farthest southwest, Northern Kyūshū (known to the Japanese as Kita Kyūshū), in 1963 was actually made up of an amalgamation of five smaller cities ranging in population from 100,000 to 300,000 (Yawata, Tobata, Wakamatsu, Kokura, and Moji). In 1985, Northern Kyūshū, center of steel production since the establishment of the government-initiated works at Yawata in 1900, had a population of just over 1 million.

Even this description of population concentration in DIDs may be misleading, for, by the late 1960s, urban settlements in the Pacific corridor reached toward each other in a discontinuous conurbation. By then all important points between Tokyo and Kyūshū had been linked by New Tōkaidō line (Shinkansen) bullet trains. A businessman could leave any point between Tokyo and Ōsaka in the morning, arrive at any other point between the great cities, and return the evening of the same day. Japan's urban phenomenon began to attract the attention of those who had coined the term *megalopolis*, and soon reference was being made to the Tōkaidō megalopolis or to Nihonopolis.[4]

Their Resources

It is a pity that Japan is so rugged and beautiful—at least in places not yet subject to environmental disruption—and is at the same time so poverty-stricken in raw materials needed for the industry built up in the megalopolitan areas. Of course, Japan is not totally without natural resources. In fact, the country enjoys two major blessings: scenery and water.

To some extent even Japan's famous scenery has been defiled. In climbing season, Mt. Fuji is littered with trash over ash. In other famous spots, garish restaurants, inns, and souvenir shops compete for space. Parking lots are jammed with sight-seeing buses, engines idling and exuding fumes. There are hordes of dedicated tourists, including bands of schoolchildren in their uniforms. Even so, there are still remote, quiet retreats with great natural beauty. Hokkaidō remains largely unspoiled with sparkling lakes, volcanic cones, isolated beaches, and deep forests. Nara is still impressive, especially at dawn.

Water is Japan's only seemingly limitless natural resource. Abundant rainfall, together with careful management, maintains green forests over two-thirds of the country's area; as a consequence, Japan remains a leading wood-producing nation of the world. Even so, more than half of the voracious domestic demand must be met by imports.

The river bottoms supply limestone, clays, and sand, so production of cement (almost 70 million metric tons a year) is no problem.

Coal, once the rationale for locating cities in northern Kyūshū and southern Hokkaidō, has been reduced to that found in poor, thin veins. Recently, two-thirds of the demand has been supplied by imports. Railways have long since been converted to electric or diesel power. In Japan's industries and homes, coal has been displaced by petroleum and natural gas.

It has become a fact of life that more than 99 percent of the supply of petroleum products must be imported. This means that some 12 percent of Japan's total imports comes from the Middle East, particularly from Saudi Arabia (Japan ranks behind the United States at 18 percent). In recent years Japan, even more than the United States, has become supersensitive to "oil shocks," to the ebb and flow of petroleum to Japan, and to the need to supply technical assistance to the Middle East.

Japan lacks all vital minerals for industry, other than sulphur. Once an exporter of copper, the country must now import 83 percent to meet industrial needs.

In this way, too, the Japanese landscape has proved to be fragile. As industrial growth in the 1960s dominated all governmental policy, so, too, dependence on imports determined Japan's international politics and domestic plans. There were, in the words of the Club of Rome, "limits to growth," and the Japan of the 1970s approached those limits. The mood reflecting subtle shifts toward the new kinds of growth in the 1970s and 1980s is dealt with in later chapters.

2

The Japanese Tradition

Until recently it had generally been believed that Japan's earliest written histories, *Records of Ancient Matters* (*Kojiki*, 712) and *Chronicles of Japan* (*Nihon Shoki*, 720), were compilations of an oral tradition. Archaeological sites currently being excavated around Nara have, however, demonstrated that written histories being prepared for emperors in the eighth century covered myths and legends, it is true, but also actual events reaching back several hundred years.

In January 1988 an ethnological museum in Chiba Prefecture announced an important discovery concerning an ancient sword that was unearthed a decade earlier: The weapon was found to be inlaid with *Chinese* ideographs in silver. Researchers dated the sword back to the middle or late fifth century.

In several ways the discovery was significant. First, the archaeological find served to remind Japanese that their documented history began at a rather late date compared with that of China. Historians pointed out that the sword could have been brought to the Kantō from the Kansai region, specifically from the area around Nara, which later (in the eighth century) became the first capital. Indeed, it could have been imported originally from Korea. In either case, it was apparent that a culture that used Chinese characters had spread more rapidly and to more remote areas than was previously thought possible.

Second, such clearly identifiable remains (and others like the sword) have tended to convert into history some of the earliest Japanese legends.

Third, many finds have clearly shown that in the very beginning of Japan's historiography, the Japanese had already been using a borrowed language for some time. For example, Ōno Yasumaro (died 723) probably prepared the first written histories and he wrote them in Chinese.

Finally, research on early materials opens up the oldest and most persistent problem in presenting the history of Japan today. Shall we emphasize the long, slow effect of domestic culture change on Japanese tradition? Or shall we concentrate on the regular impact of culture contact—from ancient times to the present—on the seemingly over-whelming influences from abroad?

ORIGINS

For many years it was assumed that the origin of human habitation in Japan substantially postdated the appearance of the island chain, that is, Japan's physical separation from the continent. The earliest accepted dates were about 4000–3000 B.C., and the first human beings were believed to have come from the continent, perhaps by way of the Korean peninsula, but definitely across water. The culture of these people was already "advanced," since they produced polished stone tools and an artistic clay pottery. It was, in other words, "external."

Archaeological Evidence

In 1949 startling discoveries were made at Iwajuku, just north of Tokyo, in a site that was subjected to scientific dating techniques. The results set back the edge of history of human life on the islands. The finds included rough stone-chipped tools of a certainly mesolithic, possibly paleolithic, era before 8000 B.C. Archaeologists believed they had un-covered evidence of ancient, organic evolution of culture on the islands, in sharp contrast with the assumption that frequent ethnic migrations from the continent produced the ancestors of the Japanese.

Another find, first opened up in 1962 at Lake Nojiri in the mountains of Nagano Prefecture, was even more dramatic. Stone implements of the Pleistocene age (anywhere from 50,000 to 1 million years ago) were found alongside interesting animal remains. The tusk of a Naumann elephant had obviously been carved by humans. And the presence of so large an animal suggested the possibility that a land bridge had provided a crossing from the continent. If this were the case, then the labels "external" and "internal" were meaningless.

To return from prehistoric mists, evidence of a neolithic culture in Japan has been clearly documented in archaeology. More than one hundred skeletons, animal bones, pottery, and shell mounds have revealed a people engaged in making household utensils, dependent on the sea around Japan, and not yet involved in agriculture. This first identifiable Japanese way of life has been called "rope mark" (Jōmon) culture, the name derived from the most remarkable Stone Age pottery in the world, a kind not turned on a wheel but impressed by a rope. Jōmon apparently lasted from about 8000 B.C. to about 300 B.C., when it was displaced by a superior culture.

So sharp was the break between prehistoric (Jōmon) and proto-historic (Yayoi, named after a discovery site in the Kantō Plain) that it has been generally assumed that this transition included massive influence from the continent. At this historical layer, polished stone tools, woven cloth, and pottery turned on a wheel were uncovered, as well as evidence that many Japanese had turned from the sea to the land—from being fishermen to being agriculturalists. Iron implements were found alongside bronze, indicating a rapidly changing technological base. The outstanding contribution of the period, which lasted from about 300 B.C. to A.D. 300, was the growth of wet-rice culture. From that point on, evidence of a Japanese lifestyle can be derived from other sources as well as archaeology.

One does not have to dig beneath the surface to find the remains of the next (semihistoric) stage in Japan's development. Scattered throughout western Japan are tumuli, hill-tombs doubtless used as mausolea, sometimes called dolmen. Some, like one in the Kibi area of Okayama in the Inland Sea region, are small; but one is half again as long as the biggest Egyptian pyramid, 360 yards (329 m) long, 30 yards (27 m) high, and built in an unusual keyhole shape. Alongside are found interesting clay figures (*haniwa*) of men, animals, and horses, and also the long sword, the Chinese Han-style mirror, and the curved stone called *magatama*. These last three were to become the imperial treasures, regalia of an emerging court.

These important finds indicate clearly that by semihistoric times (tomb culture lasted from about A.D. 300 to 750) Japan was inhabited by a culturally homogeneous folk. Despite their mixed ethnic origins, the residents were unified in culture and in language. It is also apparent that the cultural center of gravity had slowly shifted from extreme western (Kyūshū) to central Japan (the Yamato basin near present-day Nara). One theory has it that sometime between A.D. 200 and 500 Japan was permeated by Korean influence. The huge mounds indicate an organized labor force, with wealth and power concentrated in the hands of a mounted military aristocracy. The first written account, which described these people at a slightly earlier stage, is to be found in Chinese dynastic histories dating from about the third century A.D.

Chinese Accounts, Japanese Legends, and History

Although Chinese accounts prepared at the time of the Wei dynasty (A.D. 297) gave explicit directions on how to get from China through Korea to "Yamatai," they were somehow garbled, so that the destination could have been either in Kyūshū or in the Kansai region (east of present-day Ōsaka). The Chinese wrote that the islands were made up of the land of Wa (the ideograph for dwarf), which was populated by a "hundred" (perhaps meaning many) clans and that these were ruled by an empress. The Chinese account of a matriarchy must not have been far off the mark, in light of the emergence of the cult of the Sun Goddess in Japan.

Meanwhile, within Japan an oral tradition was evolving, ideas to be denounced as "mere legends," but which, just before World War II, were revived to play a key role in extreme nationalism and a disastrous militarism. They have, however, always been recognized as important because of the light they shed on early customs, habits, styles, and attitudes. Although first written down in Chinese (in the *Kojiki* and *Nihon Shoki*), they illuminated an indigenous Japanese tradition, which was then embellished with Chinese ideographs and concepts. Obviously, they also represented an important transition from primitive, oral myths about origins to sophisticated, written techniques of governmental control. Few Japanese today have read the manuscripts containing these legends in their original language. Just before the war, Japanese schoolchildren learned the stories from "civics" textbooks, which were required reading.

After an account of the myriad (six generations) of deities, including Izanagi and Izanami, the story concentrated on their child, the Sun Goddess (Amaterasu Ōmikami). She in turn ordered her grandson, Ninigi, to descend from "the plain of high heaven" to "the land of luxuriant rice fields," bestowing on him the imperial regalia. According to the legend, it was his great-grandson, Emperor Jimmu, who traveled east through the Inland Sea, conquered aboriginal tribes, and settled in the province of Yamato. In the seventh century A.D. historians calculated his enthronement to be the equivalent of February 11, 660 B.C., which became the date for Foundation Day. In these legends, too, the chief figures of an indigenous cult appeared, later to be given the Chinese ideographs for Shintō.

In the indigenous cult, anything or anyone regarded as "superior" (*kami*) was worshipped. Far more important than ancestral—even abstractly political—deities were the mundane but superior forces faced by people in a simple, agrarian society: the mountains and the streams, the fields and the forests, the big wind and the torrential rain, earthquakes and fire. In this sense, Shintō was, as Sir George Sansom put it, not a system of thought or even a religion but "an expression of national temperament." Langdon Warner called the cult the "nurse of the arts."[1]

Eventually, in the seventh century A.D., more sophisticated ideas swept in from China and helped to formalize Shintō. Later it became a state creed. Even in prewar Japan, however, one could distinguish between an original shrine cult and the evolved state Shintō. Today Shintō still plays a ceremonial role—in festivals that are expressive of village solidarity, in rituals surrounding weddings, and in dedication services used, for example, to launch a supertanker.

Beyond ritual, the original legends now occupy a position similar to that of the Arthurian cycle in British lore. There is one difference: The Japanese legends draw on different and overlapping cycles of stories. One at the core was a series of tales told by tribes in the Yamato district. Another, a more primitive set, was passed along by seafaring peoples of northern Kyūshū. Yet another was a cycle revolving around ancient Izumo (modern Shimane Prefecture), obviously a center of power competitive with Yamato. One set involved Emperor Jimmu and his expedition. Finally, most mysterious of all was a cycle of tales told by folk from the southern seas around Indonesia.

When we combine the evidence of archaeology, hints from the legends, and descriptions from written accounts, we can then begin to divide Japanese history into periods (as in Table 2.1). First is a very broad division into deduced prehistory, derived semihistory, and documented history. Under the last are subdivisions set off to reflect the style and location of political power. Selection of such a scheme of periodicity has two advantages. First, it applies terminology used by the Japanese themselves. Second, it uses specific dates. The chief disadvantage is that such sharp divisions reflect only political history, whereas social and economic changes must have moved at a more glacial pace.

The chart also illustrates our dilemma in choosing between slowly evolving *internal* development and the quickly felt *external* influence. From one point of view, usually that of outsiders, there are certain crucial dates: A.D. 645, time of the so-called Great Reform (Taika) and the beginning of overwhelming Chinese influence; *1549–1638*, the "Christian century"; *1853*, the "opening of Japan"; *1868*, the Meiji Restoration and with it the assertion of Western influence; and *1945–52*, the Occupation—again a time of overwhelming Western (American) influence. Selection of such dates, however, demonstrates various ethnocentric approaches and reflects an external view of Japanese history.

From another point of view, usually that of the Japanese, the country went through a vital foundation period *before* the advent of Chinese influence in the seventh century. Christian influence practically disappeared *after* the sixteenth century, giving way to the flowering of indigenous Japanese culture during the Edo era. Even under Tokugawa hegemony, slow but significant changes occurred in feudal Japan *before* the arrival of Perry and the Westerners. Alternating currents of peaceful development and wartime energy profoundly affected modern Japan *before* the experiment in directed change under General Douglas MacArthur. And finally, Japan plunged into a stage of high mass consumption and growth *after* the U.S. occupationnaires had gone home.

TABLE 2.1 Periods of Japanese History

Dates	Period	Event	Characteristics
PREHISTORY			
B.C.?–8000 B.C.	Early prehistoric	Paleolithic Mesolithic	No skeletons; chipped stone tools; shellfish mounds; no agriculture
8000–300 B.C.	Middle prehistoric Jōmon	Neolithic	Human skeletons; "rope mark" pottery; no agriculture
300 B.C.–A.D. 300	Protohistoric Yayoi	Continental influence	Polished stone tools, woven cloth, wheel-cast pottery, bronze, iron; wet-rice cultivation
SEMIHISTORY			
A.D. 300–750	Semihistoric Yamato Tomb	Establishment of the Yamato state	Earth-mound dolmen; sword, mirror, *magatama*; clay *haniwa*
(645)	Hakuhō	Taika reform	Chinese influence (incl. Buddhism)
HISTORY			
A.D. 710–793	Nara	Completion of Nara	Chinese influence (incl. Buddhism)
794–1159	Heian	Completion of Kyōto	Fujiwara family dominance; dualism (civilian)
1160–1184	Rokuhara	Victory of the Taira	Taira clan dominance; dualism (civilian-military)
1185–1333	Kamakura	Victory of Minamoto	Minamoto clan (Hōjō family) dominance; dualism (military) (*continues*)

TABLE 2.1 *(continued)*

Dates	Period	Event	Characteristics
1334–1391	Yoshino	Kemmu Restoration	Brief restoration of court dominance
1392–1567	Muromachi	Unification, North & South Courts; beginning of Ōnin War	Ashikaga clan dominance; dualism (military); feudalism; civil war; the "upstart lords"
(1467)	Sengoku		
1568–1599	Azuchi-Momoyama	Oda Nobunaga enters Kyōto	Unification of Japan begins
(1549–1638)	"Christian Century"	Jesuits and Franciscans in Japan	Christian conversions
(1582)		Toyotomi Hideyoshi succeeds Oda	Unification continues
(1600)		Battle of Sekigahara	Unification completed
1603–1867	Edo	Tokugawa Ieyasu becomes shōgun	Tokugawa clan dominance; dualism (military)
(1853)		Arrival of Perry	Impact of the West
1868–1911	Meiji	Meiji Restoration	Modernization
1912–1925	Taishō	Accession of Yoshihito	Taishō democracy
1926–1988	Shōwa	Accession of Hirohito	Dualism (military); war and defeat
(1945–1952)		Occupation of Japan	Dualism (civilian-military); directed change
1989–	Heisei	Accession of Akihito	Japan, a major postindustrial democracy

Once again, these developments illustrate the basic problem of discerning the admixture of a strong indigenous nonabsorbent core of Japanese culture, which is like igneous rock, and the strong external layers of alien culture, which are like sedimentary deposits. Even today, outside observers state that Japan demonstrates the universal principle of "convergence," flowing steadily toward the model of the technologically advanced society. Japanese meanwhile continue to stress the *Yamato damashii*, the original Japanese spirit, the traditional, and the unique.[2]

ANCIENT JAPAN

What the archaeological finds, the Chinese descriptions, and the Japanese legends indicate is that Japan early had a hierarchical society, that is, one arranged according to rank; leaders exercised strict discipline and levied severe punishments, especially for crimes against the group; there were taboos, primitive rituals of a protoreligious character, and a solar cult, which probably predated worship of the Sun Goddess. The society was still relatively primitive, consisting of semiautonomous tribal clans (*uji*) and functional guilds (*be*). There now seems little doubt that Jimmu was an early culture hero, a historic figure who was a contemporary of Julius Caesar. By about the sixth century A.D., a group centered in the Yamato district had established hegemony over much of southern and western Japan.

Culture Contact

Meanwhile, Japan was feeling the effects of contact with the continent by way of Korea. Since about A.D. 370, Japanese had been traveling to a beachhead at the tip of Korea called Mimana. Techniques of metal work, weaving, and tanning were brought into Japan from Korea. Sometime later Chinese ideographs were imported. These complicated little vehicles carried ideas about medicine, astronomy, and the calendar as well as new concepts embodied in Confucianism and Buddhism.

Discovery of an advanced, sophisticated culture in China had an immediate effect on Japan. What followed, according to Edwin Reischauer, was the world's first program of study abroad as Japanese youth went off to the Chinese capital at Ch'ang-an (modern Sian) to study art, science, philosophy, architecture, law, and administration. The Japanese soon revealed a passion for learning, adopting, and adapting foreign ideas to their own use. It was a matter of conscious, organized study and catching up, a path that was to be followed to some extent in the sixteenth and to a larger extent in the nineteenth and twentieth centuries.

Most significant among the imports from China were two quite different systems of thought. They were imported in somewhat the reverse order than they had developed on the continent. One, Buddhism, was a religion that was profoundly to affect Japanese national character. The other, Confucianism, was an ethic that was to provide a pattern on which Japan modeled its society.

In March 1959 Japan issued a deep red 10-yen postage stamp showing a map of Asia with stripes of light radiating from the lower left corner from India across Southeast Asia, China, Korea, and Japan. The commemorative stamp celebrated the Asian Cultural Congress held in Tokyo to mark the twenty-five-hundredth anniversary of the death of Gautama Buddha. It also symbolized fourteen centuries of Buddhist influence in Japan, sometimes violent but more often compassionate and soothing.

In the mid-sixth century, struggles over the new religion involved not only vested interests in the form of sacerdotal privileges, but also the advantages and disadvantages of adopting Chinese ways. The Soga family, Japan's first modernizers, sponsored the alien ideas and techniques. More practically, by about 587 the Soga saw to it through intermarriage that their blood flowed in the veins of the most prominent—what was to become the imperial—clan. Later, leadership was grasped by a shadowy figure, Prince Shōtoku, who probably served as a regent in the early seventh century. He organized missions to China, began to draft regulations, and launched Japan's first (Chinese-style) central government. His activities culminated in the reforms of the mid-seventh century. Prince Shōtoku built a chain of Buddhist temples linked to the great seminary at Hōyūji.

Even after the decline of the Soga, a generation of reformers continued the borrowing and the innovation with vigor. They successfully blended the indigenous cult, Buddhism, the Confucian ethic, and some Chinese Legalism.

In Japan, a community-centered lifestyle was closely connected with rice culture, in which the Japanese, like the Chinese, participated. The Japanese were prepared for the Confucian emphasis on the group. In their approach to the imperial family, they came to twist into a somewhat more literal meaning what the Chinese used as a figure of speech. The Japanese emperor's role was to be that of a symbol (whereas the Chinese emperor was an operating administrator). In Confucian doctrine as applied in both countries, administration could be moral or it could be immoral; it could never be amoral. In China, the Confucian classics and examinations based on them provided means for recruiting an elite; in Japan, hierarchy was rooted in pedigree. Thus, basic Confucian beliefs were restated and served to underline native Japanese practices. The Japanese came to believe that

- the *community* was *more important* than the individual
- the *emperor* was the font of *benevolent government*
- *ethics, religion,* and *politics* were *one*
- *all men* were created by nature *unequal*

In the year 645, about the time the Roman Empire was disintegrating into anarchy, the reformers began the restructuring of Japanese government along Chinese lines. The objectives, had they been fully realized, would have resulted in nationalization of all land; centralization of administration; registration of all subjects; and taxation by the central government. These plans were later called the Great Reform (Taika).

Although Japanese institutions ware not completely remodeled along Chinese lines, the Taika and reforms that followed in the early eighth century did move Japan up one notch on the ladder of integration as a nation-family. Japan thus embarked on its first modernization project, one of several attempts to accommodate superior alien techniques to familiar indigenous conditions. The country was never to be quite the same as it was in ancient Yamato. It was transformed from a collection of primitive tribes into an adopted member of the great Confucian family of nations. The nation-family did not, however, turn its back on its roots. Japanese made a clear distinction between borrowed and native elements. They threw away nothing.

Previously, members of one clan in the Yamato basin had played various roles: those of culture hero, high priest, and middlemen between the folk and the gods. Now this clan (it had no family name, for in legend it was *the* imperial family), with its attendant court, was used to legitimize political power through legend and religious sanction. The emperor became known as Son of Heaven (Tenshi), and more frequently, Sovereign by Heaven (Tennō); his slogan (which borrowed a Chinese slogan) was "Under Heaven—One Household."

In this earliest form of Japan's central administration (which has been called worship-government), the emperor's role was symbolic. He was withdrawn, as much as was possible, from day-to-day administration and served to legitimize the political power exercised by other families behind the "screen." Unique to the Japanese pattern of administration was this imperial institution, which already presented itself ornately wrapped in mystical robes and wearing a mask of legend, like the protagonist in a Nō drama.

Two Cities

The establishment of Nara as the metropolitan capital in 710 clearly symbolized the opening of a new era. Nara (then called Heijō-kyō) was a monument to the idea that a respectable nation should have a grand capital city. It witnessed a continuing flood of Chinese influence. Although the imperial court was to remain there only eighty-four years, this was a formative period and the city lent its name to an era.

Whereas Ch'ang-an was almost completely destroyed, Nara has survived and stands as a tribute to China's great T'ang dynasty (618–907), the exemplar for all of East Asia. The Japanese capital was laid out in gridlike fashion, much like (but a little smaller than) Ch'ang-an, in an area 9 square miles (23 km²). Nearby Hōryūji was erected (now the oldest wooden building in the world). On a larger scale, Tōdaiji in Nara proper was built to house a 53-foot tall (16 m) Buddha, still the largest bronze statue in the world. Also in the capital was built the Shōsōin, a simple but elegant log warehouse containing the collection of artistic, ceremonial, and personal belongings of the emperor who built Tōdaiji in 752. One art historian has described this heritage as similar to what the West would enjoy if the treasures of Charlemagne had been preserved intact and carefully cataloged.

According to legend, surrounding spirits did not treat old Nara kindly. Concretely, the capital was threatened by increasingly powerful and independent Buddhist monasteries. As a result, a new city, the Capital of Peace and Tranquility (Heiankyō) was built in 794. It, too, lent its name to an era, the Heian, which lasted for four centuries. Better known as Kyōto, it was the seat of the imperial court for almost 1100 years. (Even today it remains the traditional capital.) By the year A.D. 1000, Kyōto boasted a population of a half million, exceeded in size possibly only by Muslim Cordoba and Byzantine Constantinople. Some conception of the grandeur of the old city can be obtained today from the handsome Imperial Palace (reconstructed in 1854 after a fire). Japanese nationals often wait patiently for a year or more before receiving permission to enter the palace. Citizens of Kyōto, however, can visit the precincts once a year, when authentically dressed wax figures of Heian nobility are placed amidst the silently overpowering architecture.

The Heian era was marked by further Chinese influence, but the flood had been reduced to a trickle by about the ninth century. Meanwhile Heian court life was luxurious, elegant, fashionable, and detached from real life. Literature flourished, as we shall learn, but also indicated a steady decline in the power of the court. On the world scene, the refined culture of Kyōto was scarcely duplicated until the time of the Medici in Italy.

Culture Change

A traditional view of Heian Japan was given by Sir George Sansom:

Indeed the history of the seventh, eighth, and ninth centuries in Japan might well be written as a description of the building up of institutions after the Chinese model and then their gradual decay as they were displaced or smothered by a luxuriant growth of indigenous devices.[3]

The metaphor almost suggests a Buddhist image, the growth of the lovely lily out of the slime of a pond. However, did Sansom want to emphasize the decay or the luxuriant growth? John Whitney Hall of Yale University has given us another version of this history: the era marked less an experiment doomed to failure, in imitation of T'ang China, than a quiet social revolution that produced new forms of military-aristocratic administration.[4]

For 200 years, between the seventh and ninth centuries, Japan progressed. The capital, a large and impressive metropolis by any measure, thrived. The area under cultivation expanded to the limits of Kyūshū in the south and beyond the Kantō Plain to Sendai in the north. From the mid-ninth century until the middle of the twelfth century there were only minor civil disturbances.

Nonetheless, several developments took the Japanese in a direction quite different from the Chinese. First, the Japanese lacked the imperial, administrative experience developed over several centuries by Chinese even before the T'ang dynasty. Second, a strong sense of heredity, applied at the local Japanese level, persisted and barred adoption of something like China's meritocracy. Third, the Japanese lacked the spirit and the dynamic of an occasional rebellion, which regularly brought new blood into China's elite.

One of the most significant adjustments of the Chinese model was a further fissioning of the Japanese polity, setting to one side the immaculate reigning symbol (the emperor and the court) and to another the ruling instruments (of practical administration). The process was well illustrated by the predominance of the Fujiwara family from 857 to 1160. This clan married off eligible daughters to the imperial family. Clan members manipulated affairs from a position they perennially held, the post of regent. Thus appeared the peculiar Japanese brand of dualism, in this instance, civilian in character.

In fact, the Fujiwara simply institutionalized the tradition begun by the Soga and the Taika reformers. The Fujiwara in turn set a precedent followed by the Taira family and, later, by the Minamoto clan in Kamakura. The Ashikaga family was to carry on the tradition in the Muromachi district of Kyōto. And finally, the Tokugawa family raised the tradition to its highest peak, in the form of military dualism.

One of the clearest illustrations of Japanese capacity to absorb imports and adapt them was the further development of Buddhism in the countryside. This religion had all but disappeared in the country of its birth, India; in China the revival of native ideas had relegated Buddhism to secondary status. All the more amazing, then, that during the Nara and Heian eras it emerged as a strong, thoroughly naturalized unique body of religious thought in Japan.

At first, the intelligent but illiterate Japanese doubtless found it hard to grasp the abstruse doctrines of Buddhism: the dialectics of negation, enlightenment through the mind, the metaphysics of the whole, and law. But the central idea that the world revolves in a cycle of birth, death, and rebirth was not so difficult to understand. Inevitably man faces suffering. He can escape by searching for nirvana, which is not nothingness, but rather the absence of desire and, thus, the absence of suffering. In the doctrine of karma one is conditioned by what has gone before and one conditions what comes after. Thus the present is both child of the past and parent of the future.

At first Buddhism was an esoteric religion of state. As such, however, its religious fervor was expressed in tangible form—the magnificent temples, monasteries, and sculpture—and by real people—scribes, artisans, carpenters, and decorators. The clergy taught Japanese to build local temples, highways, bridges, and irrigation works. Thus Buddhism added to both the intangible and the tangible wealth of Japan. The religion became less and less like the original doctrine, which had been imported as a political instrument, and more and more like a salve, healing life's wounds.

Distinctive Japanese sects of Buddhism began to appear: for example, the Tendai group, with an establishment on Mt. Hiei near Kyōto, and the Shingon sect of Mt. Kōya just south of Nara. Soon there were political disputes. From the ninth to the sixteenth centuries, Buddhist armies repeatedly descended on hapless Kyōto, overawing the court with moral suasion and military menace. The growth of manorial estates and the rise of a new military power to defend them were in large part a reaction to the establishment of temples, and the results proved fateful.

Another clear indication of the emergence of a distinctive Japanese style lay in the appearance of new social and economic institutions. Out in the provinces, peasants began to drift to estates—really small manors (*shōen*) at this stage—offering their lands in return for protection. A typical manor was a tract of land, often newly brought under cultivation, under the patronage of an influential person or institution (for example, a courtier, a Shintō shrine, or a Buddhist temple); it had a claim to, or enjoyed, fiscal immunity. This complicated system gradually supplanted Chinese-style nationalization and paved the way to a loose form of feudalism.

The key figures in the system turned out to be neither the cultivators at the bottom nor the legal protectors in the court at the top, but local managers. They in turn came to depend increasingly on local bands of warriors, literally called "servants" or *samurai,* in a leader-retainer relationship. It took the ever-widening economic base of the estate to support this growing class of nonproducers. The warriors came to join wider alliances, which were opportunistically formed or dissolved. The elaborate Chinese-style bureaucratic positions and attendant ranks at the center remained, not as instruments of power, but as symbols of ritual and court prestige.

The Fujiwara family reached its peak of power in the late eleventh and early twelfth centuries, but by then it was pouring its considerable resources into the bottomless pit of capital politics. Meanwhile, two dominant provincial clans were laying down far firmer foundations at the local level. Eventually, the court found itself trapped as it was forced to ask first one, and then the other, clan into the capital to preserve order.

One of these clans was the Taira (also known by the Chinese pronunciation of the name, Heike), who built its power base around the Inland Sea and first entered Kyōto. The other was the Minamoto clan (also known as the Genji), who operated from the Kantō in the north and remained aloof after victory. Every Japanese schoolchild knows about the exploits of these military coalitions, if not through the histories,[5] then by way of modern novelized versions that rank as best-sellers, sword-play movies, and television dramas.

For a time, the cloistered emperor and his Taira supporters emerged victorious and dealt harshly with the rival Minamoto. The Taira ruled from a palace at Rokuhara in Kyōto (thence the name of an era, 1160–84). By the spring of 1185, the Minamoto had rebounded, gradually gained control of much of Japan, and wisely husbanded their strength around a new stronghold in Kamakura. It was a triumph of military government over civil bureaucracy, the cruder Kantō over cultured Kyōto style. A term that literally means "tent government" (*bakufu*) was applied to the Minamoto headquarters in 1190. In 1192, the leader of the clan, Minamoto Yoritomo, received the title of *shōgun* (originally, *seii taishōgun,* literally "barbarian-subduing generalissimo," who protected the frontiers for the emperor). Meanwhile, Kyōto had become engulfed in fires, plagues, and famine.

Despite Kyōto's decline, even today something of the delicate, feminine Heian culture remains in the Japanese spirit. It competes with the vigorous, masculine samurai ethos inherited from Kamakura.

FEUDAL JAPAN

For seven centuries after the victory of Minamoto Yoritomo, Japan was to be administered under a military dualism. The emperor at Kyōto continued to be the de jure sovereign, with all of the attendant court ranks and privileges. The de facto administration was located in a military headquarters, the *bakufu;* power remained in the hands of a military dictator, the shōgun. At the truly local level, certain social and economic arrangements paralleled those we commonly associate with Western feudalism. A discussion of the appropriateness of the term is best postponed until after a summary description of the Japanese variety.

Kamakura Feudalism

At Kamakura the Minamoto clan established a simple, direct warriors' administration. In their semipublic, semiprivate regime they maintained a characteristic lord-vassal relationship with their followers (and thus, some would argue, took the first step toward organized feudalism). Yoritomo did not bestow fiefs, however, and he did not replace the old civil administration. Nor was the system centralized (as much as the later Tokugawa hegemony would). The Minamoto controlled only about one-third (twenty-two) of the total number (sixty-six) of provinces. Estates were redistributed so the Minamoto-appointed stewards were grouped under the watchful eyes of protectors. The headquarters began to apply simple, customary local law (in contrast with the complicated Chinese-style codes).

The Minamoto left the court and aristocracy in Kyōto intact, but the imperial estates and nobles' holdings were carefully supervised by warriors loyal to Kamakura. Minamoto Yoritomo thus provided a bridge between two classes: The first, the hereditary aristocrats, remained haughty toward the untutored warriors out on the provincial boundaries of Japanese life; the other, a crude, unlettered band of samurai, was fiercely proud of its martial heritage and quite pragmatic in its approach to life. Increasingly, military prowess rather than birth and genealogy determined the status of these upstart lords. Nevertheless, it curiously remained a definite asset for the local figure to be able to point back to (even a fictional) high station. Moreover, the post of shōgun itself became hereditary. As Minoru Shinoda has pointed out, the Kamakura headquarters felt the need to balance traditional imperial and feudal institutions. Above all, the crux of the feudal condition, the military tie stregthened by grant of land in fief, did not appear until later.[6]

Some amazing developments in the Kamakura era symbolized the Japanese penchant for diffusion and indirection in government. The emperor continued to reign in Kyōto, but he had delegated courtly administration to a Fujiwara regent. The Fujiwara on occasion lost control of the court to descendants of a retired emperor. Meanwhile, administrative power had in theory passed into the hands of the Minamoto shōgun at Kamakura. By 1213 the Minamoto clan had in practice delegated administrative power to the Hōjō family (related to Yoritomo's wife of Taira descent). The Hōjō adopted the formal title of regent to the shōgun.

Undoubtedly the greatest contribution made by the Hōjō regents was the codification of land law. Their legislation replaced the atrophied codes inherited from China and became the predecessor to later military house laws. A military class was thus setting standards for the entire society. Its outlook was of the greatest importance.

Whereas the Heian era was one subsequently identified with high culture, literature, and the arts, the Kamakura period was one in which the way of the warrior (*bushidō*) predominated. The code has generally been compared with chivalry in medieval Europe, but the thrust was really quite different. A slogan of the samurai was, "Death is lighter than a feather, but duty is weightier than a mountain." Rather than submit to shame—arising in most cases from failure in one's duty—the warrior was expected to commit suicide by *seppuku* (or in the more vulgar term, *hara-kiri*, literally "to slit the belly").[7]

Otherwise the samurai found solace in a new, practically Japanese, form of Buddhism. Although Zen (in China called Ch'an) was originally (and has remained) meditative, it took on meaning beyond mere contemplation in military, feudal Japan. With its emphasis on self-reliance and self-discipline, Zen became an enormously popular cult among the warriors loyal to Kamakura. (Its contributions to the world of art will be examined in the next chapter.)

Internal changes contributed to the eventual fall of the Kamakura system. New local leaders, who had once held posts as stewards under the Minamoto-Hōjō hegemony, grew stronger and were the forerunners of territorial magnates later known as domain lords (*daimyō*). The final, fatal blows to the system, however, were delivered from outside Japan.

In 1274 ships built and operated by Koreans, under the command of the great Mongol leader, Kublai Khan, appeared off Kyūshū. The some 25,000 troops were unable to gain a foothold, however, as bad weather put the fleet to rout. Seven years later the Mongols reappeared with the greatest armada the world has seen (until the invasion force mustered by the Allies in World War II). Some 4,000 ships carried an army of 150,000 men to the Kyūshū beachhead. There they fought a desperate battle with samurai for fifty-three uninterruped days. Then a sudden typhoon practically destroyed the invasion fleet and cut off the Mongol ground force. The Japanese referred to the storm as the divine wind (*kamikaze*, a term adopted again in the battles around Okinawa in 1945). The Kamakura system never recovered from the heroic defensive effort.

Although there was, in the fourteenth century, a so-called Kemmu Restoration, true restoration of imperial rule was postponed for another five centuries. For a time there were two emperors and two courts, one in the north (Kyōto), one in the south (Yoshino). Warfare continued until 1392 when a weak administration under the Ashikaga family (established in power in 1336) negotiated an end to the schism. Ashikaga rule was known as the Muromachi shogunate, named after a section in northwest Kyōto.

By the mid-fifteenth century civil war was again ravaging Japan. The violence began with the Ōnin War (1467) and lasted for almost a century. Using Chinese terminology, Japanese have called the last stages of decaying Ashikaga administration the Era of the Warring States (*Sengoku jidai*).

Despite the surface chaos, far-reaching changes were having a deep effect in Japanese society. These had to do with the power structure, methods of landholding, and increasing commercial activity. By the middle of the sixteenth century, the loose control exercised by the Ashikaga had been replaced by decentralized but locally extensive control over land and human resources by independent military lords, the daimyō. Of all the periods of Japanese history, this was perhaps the most feudal.

Indeed, if we compare the Kamakura-Muromachi experience with feudalism in Europe, we find startling similarities:

> *On the social level*, private groups of armed men were united by contracts consisting of aid and service.
>
> *On the economic level*, these groups were sustained largely on agricultural land and its produce.
>
> *On the political level*, such groups had come into existence because the previous centralized state had failed to fulfill its functions. The private bodies of men were banded together not only for security but also to perform public functions. The coalescence of public and private, according to Asakawa Kan'ichi and his successor at Yale, John Hall, was a hallmark of feudalism.[8]

Is it then, wise to use the Western term *feudalism* for medieval Japan? Yes, so long as one always takes into account cultural variables. The term becomes less a pejorative word for a backward system and more a description of a dynamic process of change. Indeed, alterations were leading inexorably to larger and larger units and to their unification.

First of the unifiers was a local daimyō, Oda Nobunaga (1534–82), who crushed most of the warring lords of central Japan. He was succeeded by his brilliant lieutenant, Toyotomi Hideyoshi (1536–98), who was, according to one historian, possibly the greatest world statesman of his century. He brought the turbulent daimyō further to heel, began to set up an efficient national administration, and encouraged commerce. Unfortunately, he mounted disastrous campaigns to invade China via Korea and died before he could be informed that his attempt had ended in failure. The work of unifying Japan was concluded by Tokugawa Ieyasu (1542–1616), who became shōgun in 1603 and laid the foundations for an entirely new kind of feudalism.

Culture Contact

Certainly one of the reasons the upstart lords were able to consolidate wider and wider domains was a distinct, if subtle, change in the state of the arts. This change in turn was at least partially a byproduct of contact with a technologically superior culture once again. This time the contact came from another direction and provided the first Japanese exchange with Europeans.

The first to reach Cipango, as the Portuguese named it, were men who sailed from Lisbon in the mid-sixteenth century. Missionaries followed, among them the Spanish priest Francis Xavier. In addition to Christianity, the aliens brought the smooth-bore musket, which to this day in Kabuki drama has been named after the remote island through which it was imported (*tane-ga-shima*). They also brought new architectural designs, which, combined with temple style, resulted in the amazing castles dotted about Japan. The gun in the hands of a commoner forecast conscript armies; castles called for new defensive strategy on the part of the daimyō.

For a time, Western mannerisms and the fad of European dress were encouraged by Oda Nobunaga. Men of Kyōto wore balloonlike trousers, long cloaks, and high-crowned hats. Many Japanese wore crucifixes. Bread (*pan*) and tobacco (*tabako*) entered the Japanese diet and vocabulary. Later the Japanese became disenchanted with the religious intolerance among Dominicans, Jesuits, and Franciscans and feared that local authorities would no longer be able to control converts. The Japanese also built up a fear of the galleons of King Philip II of Spain. By 1614 the Tokugawa shogunate had banned all Westerners, except the Dutch at Nagasaki.

Centralized Feudalism

Ancestors of the administration founded early in the seventeenth century by Tokugawa Ieyasu and based in Edo (modern Tokyo) included the Minamoto shogunate based in Kamakura and the Ashikaga based in Muromachi. Japanese have referred to these predecessor regimes as "decentralized feudalism" (a term that seems to be a redundancy). In similar fashion, Japanese have called the Edo era (1603–1867) "early modern" and the Tokugawa system "centralized feudalism" (seemingly an inherent contradiction).

Here we shall describe the Tokugawa hegemony and estimate some of the lasting effects of the experience. In Chapter 3 attention will be devoted to the cultural heritage of the period, and in Chapter 4 the heritage will be considered in a different light, in a sort of balance sheet of assets and liabilities passed along to modern Japan.

The Baku-han *System.* Perhaps Tokugawa society is described as both essentially "feudal" and "under central control" because many different historical interpretations can be so accommodated. The lords who emerged from the civil strife of the Warring States period in the late sixteenth century and clustered around the three great unifiers were the prototypes of the modern daimyō. They consolidated more and more territory into larger and larger domains.

The Tokugawa clan established their military headquarters, the *bakufu,* in a small fishing village called Edo in the Kantō Plain. The eighth Tokugawa shōgun, Yoshimune, resurrected the title "great ruler" (*taikun,* from which was derived the term "tycoon"). All of Japan was subdivided into Tokugawa-held or -controlled territory and something over 250 domains (*han*). Thus, the Japanese name for the structure, the *baku-han* system.

The domains were essentially of three types. Key areas were held by related lords, cadet branches of the Tokugawa family itself. Other strategically located domains were under the control of hereditary lords who had allied with the victorious Tokugawa before the critical battle of Sekigahara. Finally there were the outer lords who had joined the alliance after the battle that secured Japan and whom the Tokugawa scarcely trusted. So long as certain principles were adhered to and injunctions heeded, administration of local-domain affairs rested with the daimyō. He was, therefore, in his own territory, a small reproduction of the Tokugawa shōgun.

Thus, a leading family was surrounded by vassals, supported by peasants on the land, and protected by a castle. Military vassalage became increasingly more significant than blood ties. Beyond the family circle, fictive kinship included housemen and retainers. The whole system rested on patron-client ties, which have been likened to the parent-child (*oyabun-kobun*) relationship.

A territorial lord (daimyō) was defined in terms of lands assessed at so many bushels of rice (technically 10,000 *koku* or more; the *koku* was about 5.1 bushels or about 1.8 hectoliter). In other words, the assessed tax yield (*kokudaka*) served as a yardstick of status and power.

Some of the injunctions and security measures of the Tokugawa proved to be important far beyond their design. A system of alternate residence, for example, required domain lords to build elaborate residences in Edo and to keep their wives and children there. Lords then traveled regularly between Edo and their domains. The shogunate thus consciously knitted together the otherwise decentralized system. Regulations guaranteed a lively and colorful flow of traffic from Kyōto and from the domains through post towns and along established routes to Edo.

The Emperor. In one way the Tokugawa family followed in the footsteps of their predecessors, the ancient Soga reformers, the Fujiwara regents, the Minamoto warriors, the Hōjō regents, and the Ashikaga military leaders: they did not usurp the throne. The emperor remained a symbol of unity, carefully protected by the Tokugawa's Kyōto deputy operating from the Nijō Castle. The Tokugawa version of feudalism never completely smothered the smoldering embers of national identity, symbolized, for example, by the imperial tradition.

Indeed, the Edo era was marked by an inchoate nationalism, which made the restoration of imperial rule easier as well as the eventual transformation to a modern nation-state. In the Mito domain, linked with the Tokugawa family itself, the development of "national studies" helped lay the ideological foundation for the late-nineteenth-century transition.

Tokugawa Society. If the political institutions of the Edo era constututed a historical step forward toward the modern condition, the social policy of the Tokugawa regime took a step backward. The Japanese version of Confucian hierarchy included the following rungs on the social ladder (from the top down): samurai-warrior, peasent-cultivator, artisan-craftsmen, townsman-merchant. In this fashion, the Japanese completely reversed the Chinese assignment of lowest status to military men.

It should be noted, however, that quite early in the "Great Peace," the samurai-warrior became, in effect, a samurai-administrator. Nor did the other dividing lines remain completely rigid: Merchant stock married or was adopted into the samurai circle; lower samurai sometimes occupied a status below peasant-headmen; in the late Edo era, men of ability, like doctors, often achieved assimilated samurai status.

Almost all historians agree that the samurai were an elite who played a crucial role in the transition from Tokugawa to modern Meiji Japan. To some, the military overlords were an arrogant, nonproducing, oppressive, parasitic class whose values were easily translated in modern times into militarism, imperialism, and aggression. To others, the samurai became civil administrators and scholar-statesmen, in Sakata Yoshio's phrase, "the intellectual and ruling class."

Certainly education, an inherent core of the Confucian ethic, was one of the primary duties of the samurai. He was to master both the military and the literary arts. By the end of the Edo era, a majority of the children of samurai above the lowest ranks were receiving formal education in at least 200 domain academies. Granted, the curricula were largely traditional, that is, Confucian and Neo-Confucian. Nonetheless, these schools became increasingly innovative in quality of education and were widespread throughout the country. Late in the period, mature samurai-scholars traveled widely among the domains as what we would now call consultants. Young samurai began their work in their own domain; some then moved on to Edo, Ōsaka, Kyōto, or Nagasaki to master languages, medicine, and (very late in the era) Dutch studies.

Some historians have remarked that Tokugawa statesmen (under the influence of Confucian doctrine, with its physiocratic bias) thought highly of agriculture in principle but poorly of agriculturalists in practice. Nonetheless, the poor plight of the peasant in the Edo era has doubtless been exaggerated. Modern field studies have demonstrated that agricultural production increased; there was a population exchange between village and city (which has continued to the present); and urban-based commercial activity dynamically affected the countryside.

According to orthodox Confucian theory, commercial profits constituted what economists today would call "unearned increment." In practice, artisans and craftsmen ranked higher than merchants, because the former were of direct service to the samurai class. Actually, by the brilliant Genroku era (1688–1704), it was difficult to separate the contributions of the samurai and others to what the Japanese have called townsmen (chōnin) culture. Most samurai and many lords came to be financially beholden to merchants. It is quite clear, however, that during the Edo period the commercial class never seized the levers of power in what we would recognize as a bourgeois revolt.

In any case, the chōnin culture of the old castle towns, which in the Edo era became preindustrial cities, did come to dominate the lifestyle not only of the townspeople but also of the samurai. A revived Kyōto continued to be the formal imperial capital and, equally important, a center for fine handicrafts (as it is today). Ōsaka, "kitchen of Japan," became the great commercial entrepôt for interisland trade. Edo, with its large population of samurai consumers, artisan producers, and merchant wholesalers, soon outstripped both of the older cities and reached a population of over 1 million in the eighteenth century. It was very likely then, as it is today, the largest city in the world.

Tokugawa Values. Although there were a number of significant changes beneath the surface of Japanese society during the Edo era, the Tokugawa hegemony continued uninterrupted for over two and a half centuries. It was a time of relative peace, not troubles, and the country remained practically isolated from foreign influence. There was ample opportunity to work out a sophisticated indigenous lifestyle. Today, even the Japanese identify native characteristics as stemming from Tokugawa society. Though they are often attributed to the tradition of agrarian village Japan, they were just as much a byproduct of preindustrial, urban Japan.

The Tokugawa values Japanese came to believe are that

- values are achieved in groups (the family, the community, *gemeinschaft, kyōdōtai*)
- these values are endowed with an almost sacred Japanese quality and are best implemented by, or in the name of, symbolic heads of family-style groups
- individual Japanese receive a continuous flow of blessings that establish obligations—in this way individuals demonstrate morality
- social, political, ethical, and religious norms are of value only as they are valuable to the group; there is no universal (only a situational) ethic

These are admittedly traditional (some would say, feudal) values. One question worth considering is, did such values have to change before creation of a modern Japan? Put another way, can traditional values and modern society coexist? (This query is discussed in Chapter 4.)

Culture Change

The seeds of change have doubtless been described, at least by implication. These alterations have led observers to apply terms like "postfeudal" or "protomodern" to the Tokugawa system. Four different arenas of change may be singled out: They have to do with education and the level of literacy, intellectual currents and the breaking away from traditional thought, the emergence of a commercial society, and the renewal of outside cultural contact.

Enough has been said about the level of education and knowledge among the samurai elite. There was also a surprising spread of learning